the rope

two poems
by John Colburn

this book is for Aki

Contents:

but they were capitalists

1

I turned on a radio
elegant sounds filled the room
holy vibrations of planetary voice
from nothing toward nothing
long delicate sentences
improvised together
through close attention
by loving each other
by practice and devotion
shaping our mouths around
the pain in our hearts
the warming planet
the hurricane damage
illness sweeping through bodies
if there was surplus we built a wall
a trench an army a category
a dollar amount
a naval blockade
terror
the next broadcast would say
the amount had gone up
we were safer
the children needed
to be in cages

2

it costs one dollar
to view the compound
from this drone
first you watch
an advertisement
you wear a mask
against the bright
transforming light
people standing in line
shuffle and weep
for the unseen
mothers and fathers
children ask permission
to crawl from cages
easy-breezy love songs
glide between reports
sweep away
the invading confusion
the inward chorus
the atrocity fatigue

3

a boy walks out of a love song
another boy
a girl walks out
a person of both worlds
a sleeping face
a rotting body
there between us
like plastic
a spirit enters the past
declares no capital
I send this message
a wolf walks out
an ostrich walks out
a hedge fund operator
we number the days
say our days are numbered
we must buy the present
continually
with our attention

4

we say dear future
this heart of mine
declares to you
the pain of capitalism
declares to you
raw pain as belief
each time money
is deposited by
electronic pulse
into a baby
another ghost walks out
a candy wrapper
thrown into
the spirit world
you is always
the future
don't look back
put your money
into babies they say
people will do
anything for a baby
if it has a name
a certain pigmentation
and money

5

a truly unstable banking system
requires constant vigilance
light must shine through it
babies begin to float
we call out to god
bacteria could be money
it could erase us
music fell to earth
in spores
to ease the pressure
of capital
we feel conflicted
we study fruit bats
we study chimpanzees and salmon
study giant fungal systems
they're just like us we say
everyone is a capitalist after all
except ghosts
who live in a lost dimension
without money
we will send them a bill

6

I would like to help
but can you not see
by my ridiculous clothing
that I am on vacation?
now in old age why not
look at the last birds
why not perform
a sea of exorcisms
why not walk across
a big sad poem
in deep dread of love
no matter how many caged children
the hoarders sacrifice
a radio says *love is the answer*
they hold a press conference
they assure us
that drowning the prisoners
is no longer torture
what about the night
we first took mescaline
and saw what was missing
I can't see it anymore
love is for ghosts

7

they held a press conference
I am getting confused
this isn't the future
we would have to buy
cars or televisions
to stabilize
the void of terror eating us
cages no longer cages
children no longer children
it's not like the inquisition
where ghosts bloom
where terror grows
blinking red lights
the children asleep
between towers
of empty distance
terror clots our ecstatic blood
they sell us the rope
the radio plays the song
it knows everything
we give up and we kiss
there is really only capitalism
it is within us
and around us
it is exactly like god

8

we pressed our faces together desperately
we were kissing and we were kissing good
we took medicine
we wrote poems
we huddled around poems
we made beautiful to-do lists
we didn't look back
we performed an enduring radioactive embrace
for the approval
of the already dead future
we described the night beautifully
at the edge of knowing ourselves
music rang through our buildings
we tried to be for everyone
we built museums and parks
circulated recipes for marvelous pastries
obscenely photographed
giant dishes of roasted meat
we grew the meat in tiny cages
we dipped our bread in the blood
housed children in cages too
future people looked back
to our corpse
and saw in our faces
the stillness of money

9

I am now writing
in the capitalist world
dear dear corpse
night of the living
sound of crawling
toward future
as dead as anyone
a voice that turns blue
from trying not to know
the inward occasion
unsatisfied corpses
look out from
the real world of light
into a dark dream
exchange faces to watch
beautiful translucent time
hatch across our skin
hour by hour
then those hours are sold

10

like twilight entering an iris
future people say
but they were capitalists
they sold each other
sold their hours
tracked each other
sold their own panicked howl
the lit screen eating
a pocket of brightness
in a yellow leaf
they sold the light
they sold the water
placed their unsteady tongues
onto envelope seals
sent promises
to the swarming dead
each line on a page
the story of a universe
moving all through all
children woke up
and marked the light
leaking a little at a time
from under their hearts
ghosts don't buy anything

11

in the night the seas shrugged
and we dreamt
a future
we squinted toward it
we lowered the visor
kept driving
our bodies stiffened
we paid close attention
the dead driver in front of us
the song inside the road
played by a demon
then in streams and fields
on deer paths
across forest ridges
where our bodies would fall
we saw ourselves
disappear
without capitalism
we loved our dreams
we reached toward the past
those dreams evaporated
now in the night
I imagine the future
from my dreaming corpse

12

dear future
we felt trapped
the door you've gone through
we can't see it
please
the heartbreak there
this little life
family I love
our meager street
slow city park
please
this lamp
that flowerpot
the last people
my little daughter
floating there in her mama
rainy afternoon
music and backache and laundry
child in the dark waterway
I write you forever
you are born
you walk through the bubble
feel the pulsing world
you look back
enter the mind palace
watch us love little packages
of this and that
we are like snipers
at the great height of time
please tell me
did you escape

13

you look back in disbelief
bells ring
doors lock
we love to imagine
the body unbuttoning itself
like a line of surf
thank you to everyone
turning into light
my shoelace a hallelujah
right now a future ghost
holds this plastic pen
this bleached paper
I love you
thank you
for arriving by candle
at the end of a long walk
we have nothing for you
but our deaths
please take them
you shake your head

14

in the lingering exultations
of late gardens
we the destroyers
plead with sudden light
our fortifications swell
along the dry riverbed
our letters to
dear ensouled others
at the shore
alone and slack
this fucking emergency
see the caged children
(are they not cages)
what is the place
with no horizon
the cage fills
voices of future choirs
sing to ghosts
any billionaire is an emergency
global finance is terrorism
look up
look out

15

now every skull sings
to the body face down
in a bed of salt
the white future night
this corner store
broken cold
kings and queens
on the doorstep
why is life so small
this trashcan life
genocide children
left to wander
a two-way mirror
they tried to love us
but we were capitalists
they saw rain in
Kurosawa movies
and they wept for rain
found a hole in our sky
they crawled through
hell has no horizon
nothing could change

16

supernatural gentle morning
arrives
a light breeze
a few leaves
at the top of that birch
moving in prayer
I watch and turn away
time passes
earth heats its degree
insects prosper
souls flee the equator
are quarantined
left to die in cages
or gunned down
we watch them doing it
on screens
we see a stream
starry evenings
snowdrift
coral
an ancestor
we turn away
we fasten
a red string of sleep
to the space between
two beds of darkness
we grope forward
into the spirit world
love is for ghosts

inside the rope

1

They did it in Detroit
and they did it in Philadelphia
they did it in Nagasaki and again in Guantanamo
and I've done some things too.

For a while I called it a blind spot.
They called it total war and preemptive strike
and trickle down economics.

They called it repatriation.
They called it enhanced interrogation.

It was like going to the gym.
It was like a frat party.

2

Sunday downtown
a trumpet player walked up the street toward us.
A drummer.

Police cars sat nearby lights spinning.
A man dressed in a brown suit and hat
carried two feathered fans and danced a circle.

Someone held a rope on each side of the street
and people behind the rope
tried to dance their way into the street
and a few made it.

For a long time I did what was done to me.

While the brown-suited man danced
for us and for himself
even the lowest street drunk could rise up and dance too.
Even the worst husband or wife.
People found their jobs by dancing.

The man in the brown suit and feathers smoked a cigar.

The government said threat level orange.

For a while I thought I got here the 'normal' way
by taking notes and writing things down
over a period of months and then years
and by noticing auras
then I learned
there was nothing 'normal' about my life
it was perverse and malformed and cruel
though that was possibly 'normal'
in any case
as I watched the brown-suited man
a crust fell away

3

In the middle of the first night people stole
the wheels off our car as we slept in the back room.

This happens, the art gallery director said. *It's a city thing.*

The second night they stole the headlights and hood and battery.

The third night they smashed a window.

We watched the car decompose.

It wasn't our car, only a rental.

We discovered we were against cars.

That part of us sided with dismemberment
and disappearance.

4

The brown-suited man took small fast steps in a circle.

We followed the dancers and the queens and the drummers.

What type of disgusting body did I leave outside the rope?

How is the front line doing, how are they holding up?

The river of people through our lives maintains a delicate system.

A hallucination is like that, delicate.

The open sores developing beneath your bathrobe.

It's fine, as long as you can still dance.

We grew more temporary.

The once-flooded city absorbed us.

Someone said *that guy over there will fuck anything that moves*
and a stoner said *everything moves*.

The man in the brown suit and hat called out to heaven
in this moment that knows your face.

They did it in Miami to the Haitians
and they did it in army barracks in North Carolina
to kids from the Midwest.

Everybody's getting fucked over and that's why we're dancing.

And I've done some things too.

5

The man in the brown suit and hat and feathers smoking the cigar
floated on the roar of the city.

People all around him danced the same dance. They were steppers.

Because we lived in the desperate world.

We danced in the desperate street.

Cops strutted near the barricades like universe killers.

Where I lived bridges collapsed into the river
and they collapsed into our blood.

Downstream they built a whole city on our waste
and it's a better city with better dancing.

My mind got quiet before it disappeared.

It was written on leaves.

6

More fancy men appeared inside the rope.

What bird had feathers like that man had feathers?

The cops looked the other way.

They walked beside us.

Their calm faces terrified me.

Five men and one woman in their brown best and feathers of all colors.

I carried a child on my shoulders.

I lived in some of the waste; I lived in a ruin.

People on their porches and on fire escapes started dancing too.

What was that cop watching?
Whatever it was
dancing soothed it.

Nobody was going nowhere.

Some people wanted to take that waste to the desert and bury it.

Was it better to build a city for dancing on waste?

Was the mind inside the body?

Everyone wanted to know.

7

At the underpass the band stopped to play loud
          in the concrete echo
and the homeless encampment woke up.

Music moved like wind on the rippling surface of tents.
People scattered beneath the freeway began twitching.

Sleepers crawled out and they had nothing but waste
though some of them could dance.

I carried a child high above the old floodline just in case.
Cardboard beds inside makeshift tents.

They did it to the Dakota in Mankato and they did it to
          a hospital in Syria.

They did it to Fred Hampton and they did it to Pablo Neruda.

Most of the people sleeping beneath the overpass
          hadn't killed anybody.

They weren't heroes.

8

Some people took video of the dancers and sent their videos
up to the cloud.

Some people sold budweisers from their coolers for a dollar and while
they practiced their trade the sellers danced and the buyers danced
and the whole transaction was dancing.

Some of the waste in our minds surfaced. Thinking waste.

I've done some things.

People can become waste. Exploded people. Drowned people.
Broken-hearted people.

Dancing was a way out of the category.
But it isn't always.

Anti-depressant missile silo lead poisoning waste.

The brown-suited dancers moved down the street, feathers high.

Some people held the rope and some people danced and some people
played in the band and some people sold water or beer or joints and
the cops walked along trying not to have any personality at all until a
beautiful woman walked by then they hiked up their utility belts and
smiled. Just an hour ago it was a boring street and the cops owned it
and someone turned left on their way to brunch in the dazzling glare.

With my hands holding the child's legs someone could pick my
pocket but I kept dancing.

Bodies do impossible things like dreaming.
People in the homeless camp watched us go.

The parade passed through their city and they sat eating
sandwiches from Sunday mission trucks.

The child watched everything.

9

An old man began to cry as he danced.
Waste and lamentation and dancing in rubble left by ships.
Dancing through a moment of cruelty
or a feeling of potential cruelty all around.

One woman said *Oh dear, blood and beer.*

We were dancing but we were walking through the streets too.

It was written on our tears.

I would not necessarily be a better person in this city.
I had never experienced dignity.

We were raised up
by dancers and steppers and drummers.
This happened on a Sunday.
It really messes with the traffic, one artist said.

Tears were not worth much in the fantasy economy.

We turned right on MLK boulevard of course.

We did not get lost.

We started out lost and we danced obscenely and cried
and we got found in the dead-end neighborhood
with the redacted waste and human juice.

Everyone wanted to know if they were still alive.

Or if they were waste.

10

The dancers in brown suits and hats
wiped handkerchiefs over their glowing faces.

They wiped the cops off their faces for just an hour.

Even an addict could join right in.
Even a tourist.

I have been on each end of cruelty.

Which is to say I have lived in a cruel family and I have
gone to a cruel school and worked at those cruel jobs
and I have been in love.

I have tried not to have a self but there it was dancing
and holding the child overhead.

The old man wept.
Another man danced on a fire escape
and a woman passed a joint.

Remember the Sabbath day and keep it holy,
full of dread, abandoned, flooded,
crossing a bridge in our mouths
to the self.

In the beginning was the word and it made us
dance.

Even those terrible ships at the ancient port
were once beautiful oak trees.

Our dreams had to stretch their talents into the past.

11

The agent of destruction sang about falling in love
and forgetting.

No one fell in love inside the rope.

We moved our snaky prayer into the neighborhoods,
cops always one intersection ahead.

Used tire shops sparkled with the rims of rental cars
and ecstatic gossip.

It seemed impossible
in the ruins
in the buildup of waste
not to channel ancestors.

From a distance you couldn't perceive it.
It was written on pieces of waste.

They did it in Flint, Michigan, to everybody, again and again.

It was worse when they talked about it afterward on the radio. Just
bullshitting us and we stood aside or fell in love with them.

Some dancing people leaked out of the pharmacy and joined up.

Some people kept on driving; they had appointments and families
and brunches and irregular tissue samples and primal
catastrophes and indecent childhoods to drive toward.

The city had cracked. We danced at the leaking crack.
The agent of destruction surged ghostly material.

We were over falling in love. We just danced the love we had
for this street at this moment.

A few people did fall into the leaking crack
and get born and pushed around by cops
and walk at night down any street singing
songs of anatomy and repentance.

12

They're doing it right now. If I turn on the dispassionate news
I will hear the objective report of them doing it.

I've done some things. I have been the least.

Kids are monsters; kids are angels.

The child on my shoulders kicked his feet
in rhythm with the drummers.

Long dreams turned
into dirt carried away by the river.
Dreams two thousand miles long
written on waste.

The cops watched us take our last turn
into the blocked off intersection.

The crying dancing man laughed at the smoking bodies
and do you know what was at the end of the line?
More cops.
More dancing.
Floods and repentance and global crisis
and looking the other way.

A queen held up her fan.
Everyone shouted that they were alive
and touched the chaotic origin
of human presence
by flame and by budweiser.

13

I did what was done to me.
On the fourth night the agent of destruction sang.
For a while I called it a blind spot.
I treated the people I loved as waste
until I became waste.

To dance inside what they are doing
and not have fatigue
requires channeling.

They broadcast detachment from ruins.
They turned people into bodiless cravings.
From a distance you can't perceive it.
Nobody fell in love.

The brown suited man danced at the end.
His feathers sang by trembling attachment.

They're doing it in Flint, Michigan.
They're doing it in Guatemala.
Turn on the radio.
Use your ears.

All the knowledge in the Western world
up to right now
becoming one sanitized object.

www.ingramcontent.com/pod-product-compliance
Lightning Source LLC
Chambersburg PA
CBHW022107020426
42335CB00012B/862